Count Alaska's Colors

By SHELLEY GILL
Illustrated by SHANNON CARTWRIGHT

D0731236

Count Alaska's Colors

Text copyright ©1997 by Shelley Gill
Illustrations copyright ©1997 by Shannon Cartwright
Printed in Hong Kong

Library of Congress Card Number 97-66963
ISBN 0-934007-35-7 (pbk)
ISBN 0-934007-34-9 (hc)

PAWS IV
Published by Sasquatch Books
615 Second Avenue
Seattle, Washington 98104
(206) 467-4300
(800) 775-0817 (book orders)
www.SasquatchBooks.com
books@SasquatchBooks.com

Dedicated to
Sharon, Chelsea, and Charlianne
—my wonderful neighbors—
Thank you so much for all your help!
S.C.

and

Heidi, Courtney, Asa, and Tim
—100% Grade A folks—
Always right there when times are tough.
S.G.

With COLORS and NUMBERS
the animals play,
learning to count
the Alaska way.

1

One mamma BLACK bear
dozing in the dew.
She rolls over and
then there are two!
Peek-a-boo!

$$\begin{array}{r}1\\+\,1\\\hline 2\end{array}$$

2

Two **BROWN** beavers
nibbling near a tree.
Look behind the rock--
now there are three!

$$\begin{array}{r} 2 \\ + 1 \\ \hline 3 \end{array}$$

3

Three WHITE polar bears
rock and roll and roar;
dancing in the dark
are the cool fab four.

$$3 + \dfrac{1}{4}$$

Four **CINNAMON** kit fox
tease a bee hive.
Ouch! It stung me!
yelps fox number five !

$$\begin{array}{r} 4 \\ +1 \\ \hline 5 \end{array}$$

5

Five **RAINBOW** trout
performing fishy tricks,
leaping up a river fall.
Oops--there are six!

$$\begin{array}{r} 5 \\ +\ 1 \\ \hline 6 \end{array}$$

6

Six BLOND grizzly bears
in blueberry heaven.
One more snoozing,
so that makes seven!

$$6 \\ +1 \\ \overline{7}$$

7

Seven RED king crabs
eating stinky bait.
Peeking from under the pot
is crab number eight!

$$\begin{array}{r} 7 \\ +1 \\ \hline 8 \end{array}$$

**Eight PURPLE urchins
clinging to a line.
The tide comes up.
Look! There are nine!**

$$\begin{array}{r} 8 \\ +\ 1 \\ \hline 9 \end{array}$$

9

Nine ORANGE starfish
twinkle in the sand.
Number ten is hiding
underneath my hand.

$$\begin{array}{r} 9 \\ +\ 1 \\ \hline 10 \end{array}$$

10

Ten CHOCOLATE moose
admire the Milky Way.
One wanders in from the brush;
eleven leap to play.

$$\begin{array}{r} 10 \\ +\ 1 \\ \hline 11 \end{array}$$

11

**Eleven ROSY Grosbeaks
warm in the sun,
gobble berries in the snow.
Now twelve are having fun.**

$$\begin{array}{r} 11 \\ +\ 1 \\ \hline 12 \end{array}$$

12

Twelve YELLOW warblers
spiral in the sky.
One swoops low,
eleven stay high.

$$\begin{array}{r} 12 \\ -1 \\ \hline 11 \end{array}$$

11

Eleven **BRONZE** sea lions
splashing in the rain.
One heads for cover;
only ten remain.

$$11 - 1 \over 10$$

10

**Ten VANILLA dall sheep
in a field of columbine.
One stops to eat some greens,
then there are nine.**

$$\begin{array}{r} 10 \\ -\ 1 \\ \hline 9 \end{array}$$

9

Nine **GOLD** wolf pups
prowl and howl too late.
One misses dinner--
now there are eight!

$$9 - 1 \over 8$$

Eight PINK porcupines
all named Kevin
play hide 'n seek
until there are seven.

**Seven GRAY marmots
practice can-can kicks.
One kicks too high
leaving just six!**

$$\begin{array}{r} 7 \\ -\ 1 \\ \hline 6 \end{array}$$

6

**Six RUST walrus
do the jelly jive.
One rolls off his rock;
then there are five.**

$$\begin{array}{r} 6 \\ -1 \\ \hline 5 \end{array}$$

5

Five CRIMSON caribou,
feet are getting sore.
One takes a flying leap
then there are four!

$$\begin{array}{r} 5 \\ -\,1 \\ \hline 4 \end{array}$$

4

Four BLUE whales
blowing bubbles in the sea.
One dives deep.
Now there are three!

$$\begin{array}{r} 4 \\ -\ 1 \\ \hline 3 \end{array}$$

3

Three TANGERINE beaks
chirp and squawk and coo.
One puffin dives away
I see only two!

$$3 \\ -1 \over 2$$

2

Two **TAN** coyotes
melting in the sun.
The first cries, "I'm outta here!"
That leaves one!

$$\begin{array}{r} 2 \\ -\ 1 \\ \hline 1 \end{array}$$

1

One OLIVE green otter
not having any fun.
He swam off to find a friend

$$\begin{array}{r} 1 \\ -1 \\ \hline 0 \end{array}$$

Now there are none!

A triangle of TURQUOISE iceberg
drifting in the bay,
a shape with three sides
where orcas go to play.

A square made from VIOLETS
is a tasty flower bunch,
a shape with even sides
until the squirrels finish lunch.

A circle of GREEN grass,
mountain goat's delight.
A shape with no sides--
a soft bed at night.

If you're feeling frisky
and would like to take a test,
count every animal
before you take a rest.

How many critters
are romping in this book?
Some of them are hiding--
don't forget to look!

ANSWER HERE

THE ALASKA ABC BOOK

KIANA'S IDITAROD

MAMMOTH MAGIC

ALASKA MOTHER GOOSE

THUNDERFEET

DANGER – The Dog Yard Cat

ALASKA'S THREE BEARS

NORTH COUNTRY CHRISTMAS

COUNT ALASKA'S COLORS

IDITAROD CURRICULUM

SWIMMER

DENALI CURRICULUM

ADVENTURE AT THE BOTTOM OF THE WORLD

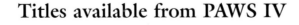

STORM RUN

Titles available from PAWS IV

Published by Sasquatch Books
615 Second Avenue
Seattle, Washington 98104
(206) 467-4300
(800) 775-0817 (book orders)
www.SasquatchBooks.com
books@SasquatchBooks.com

PAWS IV VIDEO COLLECTION